OSWALDTWISTLE OBSERVED

(Gawping at Gobbinland)

by

Mike Booth & Albert Wilkinson

Landy Publishing
2003

ISBN 1 872895 62 X

British Library in Cataloguing Publication Data.
A catalogue record of this book is available from the British Library.

Layout by Mike Clarke. *Tel/Fax: 01254 395848*
Printed by Nayler the Printer Ltd., Accrington. *Tel: 01254 234247*

Landy Publishing have also published:

Accrington Observed by Brian Brindle & Bob Dobson
Accrington's Changing Face by Frank Watson & Bob Dobson
Accrington's Public Transport 1886-1986 by Robert Rush
A Blackburn Miscellany edited by Bob Dobson
Blackburn Tram Rides by Jim Halsall
Blackburn in Focus by Alan Duckworth & Jim Halsall
Preston in Focus by Stephen Sartin
Bolland Forest & the Hodder Valley by Greenwood & Bolton

A full list is available from:

Landy Publishing
'Acorns' 3 Staining Rise, Staining, Blackpool, FY3 0BU
Tel/Fax: 01253 895678
e-mail: bobdobson@amserve.co.uk

INTRODUCTION

Our aim in presenting this book is to give, with pictures, an illustration of Oswaldtwistle (which we will call Ossy from now on) and to add comments to those images so as to interest and inform readers.

We hope that, in presenting these pages, we have shown the diversity of life and terrain in Ossy's 4,885 acres and especially in the industrial heritage. Before the Industrial Revolution (and after it too) the majority of the township was farmland, but the coming of the factories brought muck and money. Cotton spinning, weaving, bleaching, dyeing and calico printing were, from about 1820 onwards, the most common occupations, followed by coal-mining, and to a lesser degree chemicals production and engineering. Victorian Ossy was a thriving town, impregnated with the smoke from many factory chimneys. To escape it, the inhabitants needed only to walk uphill to reach *"t'tops"* where there was green grass, whinberries and countless streams.

Oswaldtwistle has been spelt in many ways over the years. One variant is recorded as far back as 1241. The whole area, then a manor in its own right in the Honour of Clitheroe, in Norman times, was probably named after St. Oswald, the hero King of Northumbria. This connection is reinforced by the fact that there was a St Oswald's Well at Church Kirk which was named in documents as early in the 13th century. *'Twistle'* is derived from *'twisla'*, a river junction.

In selecting the name for our book we sought to tell people that this was a look at the town and its folk. *"Gawping"* is a Lancashire dialect word meaning to look or stare at. *"Gobbinland"* is the place where *"Gobbins"* or *"Gobbiners"* live. For many generations, Ossy folk have been called, and with pride call themselves *"Gobbins"*. The origin of this, as with many other nicknames applied to Lancashire places and folk, is that it is a term of derision laced with humour, for a *"gobbin"* is a simpleton. Some suggest that the *"gob"* in gobbin is linked to *"gob"* meaning *"waste"* in coal mining. It is said that to be a true *"Gobbiner"* one has to have been born *"above t'lamp"*. This was erected in the 1860s by the Local Board at a spot near to where the present library is on Union Road. It would initially burn Ossy-made gas.

We declare our fervent support and heart-felt pride in the names *"Ossy"* and *"Gobbinland"*.

We express our appreciation for help received in the compiling of this book from the staff at Ossy Library, Accrington Local Studies Library; Oswaldtwistle Civic Society; Hyndburn Local History Society; the management of *"Ossy Mills"* and to numerous other generous Gobbiners and honorary Gobbiners who have loaned their photographs and given their time and knowledge.

Church & Oswaldtwistle Railway Station c1900. The railway from Blackburn to Accrington was opened on 19th June 1848 by the East Lancashire Railway. The station is actually just inside the Church boundary. The rooms above the Lancashire & Yorkshire Railway Co. sign are the Station Master's house, a far cry from today's unwelcoming, unstaffed halt. An Accrington-bound tram trundles past the station approach. The three storey building on the left, adjacent to the overbridge, was the *Station Hotel*.

Foxhill Bank Brow c1950. Foxhill Bank Printworks was associated with James Simpson in the mid 19th century and then became part of *Frederick Steiner & Company* in 1891. Hence the name Frederick Street. Frederick Steiner left Alsace in northern France and came to Lancashire in 1817. His business had been ruined by the Napoleonic Wars. Having worked at Broad Oak, Accrington he went on to produce a cheaper and quicker method for making Turkey Red dye and made himself a fortune. His daughter Emma was the renowned beauty who became a favourite of the Prince of Wales. When Edward became King he installed Emma in the *White Lodge* at Richmond Drive. The printworks continued until 1931. The sign, NEHESCO, probably denotes the company bleachworks of *Neuss, Hesslein & Kempton Limited* that operated there from 1935 to 1958.

Union Road c1900. Although denoted as Market Street this looks onto the start of Union Road. The impressive and decorative red brick and ashlar facings of the *Liverpool and Manchester District Bank* on the corner of Foxhill Bank Brow and Union Road are part of an impressive collection of late 19th century buildings that inevitably included the public house and a picture theatre, namely the *Empire*. The time taken by the photographer to set up his apparatus gave the children of Church and Oswaldtwistle enough time to gather and become immortalised in this lively picture of a very old part of Oswaldtwistle. Much of this has been demolished, though the bank and hotel still exist.

Left: **Treacle Row, Union Road c1900**. These shops on Union Road were demolished in 1907 to make way for the electric trams. The Church & Oswaldtwistle Technical School, built in 1911, still occupies this site as part of Oswaldtwistle's contribution to the promotion of education and heritage.

© *Lancashire Library*

Below: Much of this part of Oswaldtwistle was swept away in early 20th century improvements. Oswaldtwistle is well noted for its many hostelries. On the left hand sude of Union Road we find the *Fisherman's Arms* at 9 Union Road, right on the corner of Clayton Street. This no doubt provided sustenance to all those who fished in the two extensive lodges in the *Alleytroyds* area of Church nearby...

...Not much further down the road can be seen the tall building of the *Castle Inn* at 25 Union Road. Between these was the *Startled Fox* at 17. At 47 on the corner of *Moscow Mill Street* stands the *Printer's Arms* denoting the connection with the calico printworks at Foxhill. The prolific number of drinking establishments in Oswaldtwistle in the late 19th century is well represented in this example of a short stretch of the main road. Public houses provided many functions and enabled the community to exist at a time when few had a telephone. In the town centre, messages for a funeral director could be left at the *Old-House at Home* if the funeral parlour was shut. © *Lancashire Library*

Treacle Row, Union Road, c1900. This section of the road was very narrow before the coming of the tramway. The Technical School was built on the right, on the approximate site of Treacle Row. Treacle was part of the staple diet of the working classes in the late 19th and early 20th centuries and was sold from one of the shops on this row. © *Lancashire Library*

Union Road, opposite Moscow Mill Street in the early 1950s. There had been a printing firm at 56 Union Road for many years, run successively by Mr. Horrocks and Mr. Jackson. In 1920 it was bought by Ernest Nayler, Jackson's employee. *Nayler the Printer* moved to Aero Mill, Church and the buildings were demolished to become Badge Brow Service Station which has recently been demolished. This book is printed on state of the art machinery installed by the founder's grandson.

Union Road, junction with Moscow Mill Street in the 1950s. A Clayton-le-Moors bound bus stops outside the Technical School. Moscow House, built by Robert Walmsley of Moscow Mill and now a doctors' surgery, can be seen in the left distance.

St Paul's School, Union Road c1900. The school was established in 1837 by the *National Society for the Education of the Poor* in the principles of the Established Church. The row of houses opposite the school were converted to shops and subsequently demolished to make a car park. © *Lancashire Library*

A Sunday School procession passes the same location about 1912. Note the shops converted from the houses opposite the school and the widened road to allow for the construction of the tramway. Even though electricity had been provided for the tramway, gas street lighting reigns supreme.

King George V's Coronation Day Procession on June 22nd 1911. Although the members of the council were reported as travelling in landaus it is likely that these are the elected members of the Oswaldtwistle Urban District Council. These prosperous gentlemen in top hats, many of whom would be high ranking industrialists, having just passed the entrance to Busk Meadow Street convey the confident mood of the times. This year marked the heyday of the Lancashire textile industry. The prosperity of the Empire seemed assured and yet there were rumblings in the Balkans.

Coronation Day Procession; the float of the *Church & Oswaldtwistle Weaver's Association* lavishly decorated with fancy cloths. A weaver, Miss Aspinall, was part of a parade that took an hour and a half to travel the length of Union Road. 1911 was not a settled year for industrial relations in Oswaldtwistle. The strength of the unions was growing and the existence of the closed shop almost brought Moscow Mill to a lock-out when three weavers refused to join the Association.

Oswaldtwistle Urban District Council Chamber. The *Oswaldtwistle Local Board* came into existence in 1867 mainly to provide the town with gas and water services. In 1894 this became the *Oswaldtwistle Urban District Council*. In the same year the town hall was built at a cost of £5000. The Urban District Council existed until reorganisation of local government in 1974. The last town clerk, Eric Roberts, went on to serve the town as the first Chairman of the Oswaldtwistle Civic Society for many years. As an ambassador for the town he was instrumental in creating the Oswaldtwistle Heritage Centre opposite the Civic Theatre on the Straits. The society continues to promote the unique heritage of the town now part of the borough of Hyndburn.

Oswaldtwistle did not give up its independence as a separate local authority without a *'fuss'*. Plans to blockade Union Road at the boundary with Church were proposed by Councillor Clifford Walsh and were taken seriously in some quarters. A quotation for the supply of sandbags was received by the council. Eventually the inevitable had to be accepted! The proposals for further local government reorganisation may include a merger with Blackburn – bring out the sandbags and man the barricades! © *Lancashire Library*

Union Road opposite Haworth Street in the 1950s. Whilst most of the buildings on the right, including the *Horse Shoe* and *Prince of Wales* public houses, were demolished to make way for new housing, the newsagent, Post Office and the Foxhill public house and other buildings on the left still exist.

Foxhill Grove Methodist Chapel. Built in 1872, the Chapel closed in 1968. It was then used by a slipper manufacturer until the early 1990s. Sadly damaged by fire in September 1992 and demolished in 1993, the site is now a car park for the adjacent car showroom.

Oswaldtwistle Fire Brigade outside the Town Hall where the gleaming steam powered fire engine was housed. The stables for the horses were across the road behind Union Road. Previously the works of Simpsons and Steiners operated fire engines. By popular demand in 1899 the Oswaldtwistle Urban District Council provided the town with this proud addition to its services. The Council also employed a medical officer and a school attendance officer at that time.

© *Lancashire Library*

Fire Station, Mill Hill. A 1950s photograph shows the old fire station at Mill Hill. This was the former Duckworth's wheelwright shop. The adjacent house also belonged to the fire service. The fire station moved from the Town Hall to Mill Hill in November 1939. These buildings were replaced in 1976 by the now closed fire station, the fire engine temporarily returning to the Town Hall during construction works. In 2003, during the fireman's strike the Army Green Goddess fire engine was temporarily housed in Lord Street adjacent to the Town Hall. History keeps repeating itself!

© *Lancashire Library*

A contented group of regulars at the *Carters' Arms* is enjoying a drink. The pub was at the junction of Union Road and Queen Street. © *Lancashire Library*

The *Hare & Hounds* on Blackburn Road (c1912) with a coach party from Woodnook Baptist PSA (*Pleasant Sunday Afternoon*) on its way to the Hodder. Jovial PC '*Bobby*' DeVoy manages to get into the picture. © *Lancashire Library*

The first St Paul's Church was a temporary corrugated iron building, purchased second hand, erected on Queen Street and consecrated in 1870. Following construction of the present church, it was sold for £200 and re-erected in James Street, becoming the *Free Congregational Church* and, later, a Spiritualists meeting place. It was known as the *'tin tabernacle'*. In 1909 it became *Oswaldtwistle Working Men's Club* until their new premises were built in 1912. The picture shows the former *iron church* in James Street about 1910. © *Lancashire Library*

The interior of *Oswaldtwistle Working Men's Club* about 1910. It was known by the regulars as the *'tin hut'*. © *Lancashire Library*

Mule spinning at *Paddock Mill* c1920. Usually mule spinners were men and boys. They worked in bare feet and were found to be quite deft at picking up loose cotton with their toes. A good mule spinner could earn high wages as the even quality of the yarn depended on his skills. Mule spinning can still be seen at Helmshore Textile Museums. © *Lancashire Library*

Threebrooks Mill c1920. Preparation of the warp beam – '*drawing-in*' – in contrast to the noise of the weaving shed this task was quite peaceful, though laborious. Elderly gentlemen, some in their eighties, often undertook this task, sometimes assisted by a young boy, which was all part of the preparation of the warp beam. © *Lancashire Library*

Right: **Beam warping** at at *Threebrooks Mil* c1920. Winding the warp threads or 'ends' onto the warp beam. Warpers were usually women. The creels carried between 400 to 600 bobbins. Continuous winding of warp threads onto these beams on the left provide the looms with their warp threads before being sized. The larger part of the workforce at *Threebrooks* were women. Many describe being quite frightened of Mr Kastner, a large, very imposing gentleman who ran the mill like clockwork. © *Lancashire Library*

Two Oswaldtwistle weavers at *Hoyle Bottom Mill* c1910. The mill opened as a spinning mill using water power in 1785 and converted to steam power in the 1820s. Weaving was added in 1867. The mill closed in 1930 and was demolished soon after, though remains of the mill can still be seen, together with the coach house and cottages, in Hoyle Bottom. The arched recesses held tacklers' benches.

Threebrooks Mill c1920, the Warp Dressing Room. *Threebrooks* enjoyed considerable prosperity in the 1920s largely through the work of R. J. Kastner who took over the mill in 1900 trading as C. & W. Walmsley. Kastner introduced the production of coloured fabrics. The company exported to South America, Asia and Australia. *Threebrooks* was a highly successful mill throughout the 1930s. Jobs at *Threebrooks* or '*Treebrooks*' were much sought after in the years noted for unemployment and the Depression. © *Lancashire Library*

The cheese and cop dye-house or *dye shop* at *Threebrooks Mill* c1920. The success of the cotton industry resulted from the variety of colours available for this versatile material. Producing an extensive range of patterns and colours by combinations of colours in the warp and weft threads increased the popularity of cotton. Many of the 19th century check weave designs continue to this day in fabrics and furnishings for upholstery as well as in shirtings and tickings.

© *Lancashire Library*

Beam dyeing at *Threebrooks Mill* c1920. Many fabrics require the warp threads to be dyed all one colour. The variety of colours, many of them developed in the Oswaldtwistle and Church chemical works by the works of Peel, Simpson and Steiner, gave the Lancashire textile industry a vast range of colours.

© *Lancashire Library*

A charabanc outside the *Tinker & Budget*, probably about 1920. The coach party could well be a *'tacklers' picnic'*, possibly from *Rhyddings Mill*. The name *'Tinker & Budget'* refers to a tinker (an itinerant workman) and a budget, which was his bag or knapsack.

© *Lancashire Library*

Tinker Brow, Union Road c1920 showing a tramcar descending the hill, known locally as *Tinker Broo*.

Shuttleworth's Refreshment Rooms at the corner of Roegreave Road and Union Road in the early 20th century. The second man from the right is *Bill o'Bass Bob* (Walmsley). Bass Bob was a singer. Note the signs for '*Oswaldtwistle Cycle Club*' and '*Messages for Dr Fox*'. Just visible, behind the head of the third man from the left, is the fire bell which, when pressed, rang an alarm at the Fire Station in Oswaldtwistle Town Hall. Having collected the horses and raised steam for the pump, the horse-drawn engine arrived to be directed to the fire.

Union Road junction with Roegreave Road c1905. *Shuttleworth's Refreshment Rooms* are seen on the corner of Roegreave Road with Holy Trinity Free Church of England in the background.

Liberal Club Bowling Green
Oswaldtwistle.

"Opening Game"
June-20-1906.

Oswaldtwistle Liberal Club on 20th June 1906. The former Liberal Club, which still exists adjacent to the War Memorial on Rhyddings Street, was built in 1894. The building has more recently been used for offices for Shopfitters and as a doctors' surgery. The War Memorial now stands on the site of the bowling green. Pictured in the photograph are (L-R) Jas Storey, Peter Sharples, Moses Haworth and Walter Booth. © *Lancashire Library*

The War Memorial was dedicated on 14th January 1922, by Major General Stourbridge of the 42nd East Lancs Division. Financed by public subscription, it was originally dedicated to 250 men from Oswaldtwistle who gave their lives in WW1. It is built from Cornish granite and bronze. Fewer finer war memorials exist and it deserves its prominent position in the town. © *Lancashire Library*

Stanhill Village, approaching from Knuzden. Stanhill Lane takes us down towards Oswaldtwistle. Stanhill derives its name from the stone hill where quarrying for the local sandstone was an extensive industry in the 19th century. Considerable handloom weaving took place in this hamlet before steam loom weaving took over in the factories. There are still many handloom weavers' cottages in existence; though now converted they can still be recognised by traces of infilled windows.

The Post Office at Stanhill, also known as *Rose Cottage*, was the home of James Hargreaves who invented the *spinning jenny* in 1764.

Stanhill Village, Oswaldtwistle
(where the "Spinning Jenny" was invented).

String Band at *Stanhill Sermons*, probably c1910. The *Sermons* had been an important part of the social calendar since 1837, when the United Free Methodists became established there. Stanhill, at one time, elected its own '*Mayor*'.

Foxhill Bank Hall built for James Simpson and the home of the Simpson family until 1890. It was James Simpson the Younger who became the first President of the Vegetarian Society in 1847. The building has been demolished.

© Lancashire Library

Coach Road and Simpson's Bridge in 1993 following the bridge's renovation. The arrival of the East Lancashire Railway in 1848 did not please everyone. James Simpson embellished the stark and functional railway viaduct with a balustrade and niches. This helps to soften an unsightly intrusion of this crossing of the coach road from the Lodge House of Foxhill Bank Hall to Blackburn Road. Although industrial manufacturers created many eyesores it did not mean they liked them near their homes.

© Lancashire Library

Rhyddings Hall, a fine Italianate villa built by Robert Watson, of Stonebridge and Rhyddings Mills, in 1853 at a cost of £16,000. The house became a museum, but was demolished during the 1930s. Rhyddings Park, formerly the grounds of Rhyddings Hall, together with the coachman's house (Rhyddings Cottage, Fielding Lane) and the lodge house (on Edinburgh Drive) still survive as a reminder of the importance of Robert Watson in the development of Oswaldtwistle in the 19th century. It would appear that before Watson's rebuilding, the spelling was Riddings.

The opening of Rhyddings Park in May 1909 by Councillor Arthur Hargreaves of Moscow Mills, one of the main advocates of a park. The photograph shows the temporary gates to the park at the top of Rhyddings Street.

Town Bent Pit, the last Oswaldtwistle colliery to be developed by Thomas Simpson & Company in 1889-1902. Mining ceased there in 1924-25. During 1926, the year of the General Strike, Oswaldtwistle Collieries Limited went into voluntary liquidation. Remains of the coke ovens can still be seen in the gardens nearby. © *Lancashire Library*

Townebent or Town Bent; a busy settlement in Tudor times, this was the home of the Rileys of Townebent, a branch of the Rileys of High Riley in Accrington. An ancient local surname evenly spread throughout East Lancashire, the Rileys were living at Town Bent in 1575. The area was a centre for woollen weaving before the arrival of the cotton industry. © *Lancashire Library*

Higher Twinch and Lower Twinch in the distance. Situated on the banks of White Ash Brook in an isolated part of Oswaldtwistle, the name intrigues. Although the surname *Twinch* is quite common there is no real evidence of this being a local surname. The place name may derive from its situation on the twinch of higher land next to a stream or brook.

© *Lancashire Library*

The four cottages of Higher Twinch with the footbridge and sluice over White Ash Brook. The photograph was taken after *White Ash Paper Mill* was demolished in the 1930s. There were two mills; the earlier dates from 1816 and it was here that a mob in the Power Loom Riots of 1826 smashed James Bury's machines. Two of the rioters, brother and sister, Michael and Phoebe Tomlinson from Oswaldtwistle, were sentenced to death for destroying ninety four of these new power looms. Their sentences were later commuted to eighteen months imprisonment. When released from Lancaster Gaol they found employment very hard to come by on their return to Oswaldtwistle.

Aspen Lane, Stanhill. The earliest mention of the name *Aspen* or *Aspden* is in 1316 in reference to one Adam de Aspen. Lands called *Aspen* probably gave rise to the local surname Aspen or Aspden. Aspen Lane once connected Stanhill with the town's earliest place of worship, St James's Church or Church Kirk. Many of Oswaldtwistle's notables are buried in the graveyard of this fine old church. At the northern end of Aspen Lane was Aspen Colliery. The industrial activity of the 18th and 19th century dominated most of Oswaldtwistle and Church. These cottages remind us all of a more rural and slower pace of life before the industrial revolution swept through Aspen Valley.

© Lancashire Library

Stanhill Farm c1900. This stood at the junction of Stanhill Lane and Aspen Lane. *© Lancashire Library*

Rough Hey, the old homestead of the Walmsley family. It was from here that Benjamin and Robert Walmsley ventured into power loom weaving. Despite suffering losses to their enterprise as a result of the attacks on their machines during the Power Loom Riots of 1826 the brothers went on to develop power loom weaving at Moscow Mill in Moscow Mill Street. For many years Moscow Mill was always known as *Walmsleys*.

© *Lancashire Library*

Rhoden Fold c1900. This ancient homestead dates back to 1633. The dwellings and farm buildings were completely modernised in the latter centuries with the improvements in farming methods. The upright stone walling, peculiar to this part of England, still remains.

© *Lancashire Library*

Vine Mills were established in 1875 by the *Vine Spinning Company*. A second mill was added in 1899, a third in 1906/7, and the last in 1913/14. The last of the mills closed for spinning in 1968, and today a variety of small industries are based here.

© *Lancashire Library*

The spinning room at Vine Mill, with the carding machine and draw frame tenters at work.

Peele Fold: The first Peele to be identified in Oswaldtwistle is Robert Peele who bought *Oldham's Cross* in 1731 and renamed it *Peele Fold*. The '*e*' was later dropped. His grandson, Robert Peel, established the family in textile manufacturing. He also began experimenting in calico printing at this Tudor homestead. In partnership with Jonathan Haworth, his brother-in-law and William Yates, about 1760, they raised enough money to establish the *Brookside Calico Printworks*. Using a parsley pattern, the printworks developed a range of colours and designs that helped to popularize the use of printed cotton cloth in the 18th century. The nickname Robert '*Parsley*' Peel is now part of this great story of a family who went on to dominate the local calico printing industry. Sir Robert Peel, once Prime Minister of Great Britain, is the grandson of Robert '*Parsley* Peel' the man who established the family fortune from a small farm in Oswaldtwistle. © *Lancashire Library*

Robert Peel, father of the future Prime Minister, lived at Peel Fold whilst developing his textile business. © *Lancashire Library*

James Hargreaves, inventor of the *Spinning Jenny*, was an employee of Robert '*Parsley*' Peel. Born in Oswaldtwistle and baptized at Church Kirk on January 8th 1720/1, he is described as a short man, broadly built, with stiff black hair. Although poorly educated, he was an undisputed mechanical genius. He married Elizabeth Grimshaw at Church Kirk on September 10th 1740. For a time the family lived at Brookside where James was employed as a carpenter and later a bookkeeper. In 1764 he invented the now famous *spinning jenny*. This was a machine to speed up the process of spinning yarn. The name derives from his wife's village nickname, a spinner herself, known locally in this village of handloom weavers and spinners as '*Spinning Jenny*' because of her skill at the spinning wheel. Hargreave's machine was felt to threaten the livelihood of the spinners and in 1768 the machines were smashed by a mob at Brookside and also at Rose Cottage in Stanhill where the family were living by that time. Although windows and family furniture were also smashed, the home of James and Elizabeth Hargreaves still stands. (For a long time, until 2003, it was Stanhill's post office) The Hargreaves family were forced into hiding at Ramsclough and later fled to Nottingham where James Hargreaves died in poverty in 1778. His wife later received a small sum of money in recognition of her husband's contribution to the start of the textile revolution. The machine marked the transition from the homes of the spinners and weavers into the '*manufactories.*' The Industrial Revolution in cotton textiles started in Oswaldtwistle.

A steam tram engine and wagon outside the *Black Dog* during construction of the electric tramway in 1906. They had been used for delivery of materials for the new electric tramway and a crowd of locals took the opportunity of a photo call. Steam trams operated from Accrington to Church in1886 and to Blackburn in 1887. No public steam trams operated to the *Black Dog*.

Tramway pole erection for the new electric trams, at the junction of Union Road/New Lane in 1907. The horse-drawn crane used for installation is a far cry from today's hydraulic cranes.

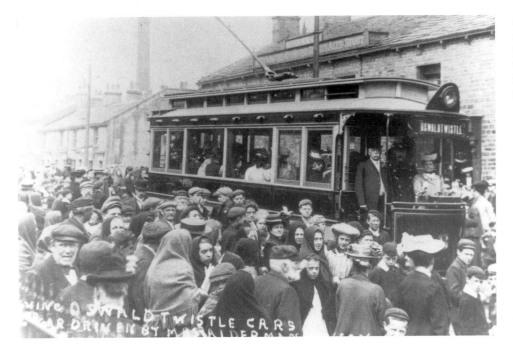

A group of tramway officials and contractors' staff pose for photographs taken at the tramway terminus at the *Black Dog* prior to the opening of the electric tramway in 1907.

Following inspection by the Board of Trade on 1st August 1907, permission was given to open the electric tramway and a procession of cars, with the Mayoress of Accrington, Mrs. A. S. Bury, driving the leading car, formally opened the tramway. The first tram is shown at the *Black Dog* terminus. A fifteen-minute service operated daily, except Tuesdays, Saturdays and Sundays, when a 10-minute service operated. The fare to Accrington was 2d (less than 1p). Also in 1907, an Accrington to Blackburn service commenced, obviating the need to change trams at Church.

Union Road, near Bent Street, 1907. The photographer was no doubt trying to take an official photograph of a tramcar on test, but, instead, he got this never to be repeated masterpiece. The policeman can be seen gently escorting this nasally challenged child to safety.

TRAMWAY GUIDE—continued.

ACCRINGTON to CHURCH and OSWALDTWISTLE.

Mon., Tues., Weds., Thurs., Fri., Sat.:—8-15 a.m., and every 10 minutes to 10-45 p.m., then 11-0 p.m.

Sunday:—9-30 a.m., and every 20 minutes to 12-50 p.m., then 1-5 p.m., and every 10 minutes to 10-45 p.m.

Workmen's Cars:—5-20, 5-35, 5-45, 6-5, 6-15, 6-25, 6-45, 6-48a, 6-50. 6-55, 7-5, 7-8, 7-15a, 7-20, 7-28, 7-35, 7-45, 7-55, 8-5 a.m.

Note.—(a)—To Church only. Cars leave Church for Oswaldtwistle about 8 minutes after leaving Accrington.

OSWALDTWISTLE to CHURCH and ACCRINGTON.

Mon., Tues., Weds., Thurs., Fri., Sat.:—8-13 a.m., and every 10 minutes to 11-3 p.m., then 11-18 p.m.

Sunday:—9-50 a.m., and every 20 minutes to 1-10 p.m., then 1-23 p.m., and every 10 minutes to 11-3 p.m.

Workmen's Cars:—5-40, 5-55, 6-5, 6-25, 6-33, 6-45, 6-58b, 7-3, 7-10, 7-15, 7-20, 7-25b, 7-28, 7-35, 7-45, 7-53, 8-3 a.m.

Note.—(b)—From Church only. Cars leave Church for Accrington about 8 minutes after leaving Oswaldtwistle.

More trams - this time on the Blackburn route. A Blackburn Corporation tram passes the *Hare & Hounds* on Blackburn Road, Oswaldtwistle, bound for Accrington, about 1910. Note the 'interlaced' track configuration, used when there was insufficient road width for two normally spaced tracks, and the decorated tramway pole.

A Blackburn-bound tram trundles past the junction of Windsor Road and Blackburn Road in the early 1940s along a fine, wide, setted roadway. The buildings in the left background (actually in Rishton) were originally the *Fountain Free Brewery*, built 1899, (adjacent to the *Mother Redcap*). By the 1930s they had become *Ribble Paints & Varnishes*. The motorway overbridge, which would appear in today's picture, was not needed to cope with the traffic in the 1940s!

Aspen Valley Viaduct, pictured about 1910, was built for the opening of the *East Lancashire Railway* between Accrington and Blackburn in June 1848. Most of the viaduct was within Oswaldtwistle. Ground conditions in the area precluded a masonry viaduct so a timber trestle bridge was constructed, 70 feet high with thirty-three 25ft spans. Infilling, to form an embankment, started in 1891, and was completed in the 1920s. Although now somewhat overgrown, the embankment can still be seen.

Lower Aspen Farm with the viaduct behind. The farm was one of the old local homesteads.

© Lancashire Library

Detail of the trestle structure of Aspen Valley viaduct. The timbers were massive and needed constant maintenance and inspection to ensure that sparks and cinders from passing locomotives did not set fire to the structure.

The fire prevention team are pictured at the Rishton end of the viaduct, where water could be pumped from the *Leeds & Liverpool Canal* to extinguish any fires along the whole length of the viaduct.

The Straits and Hippings Vale Mill.
Clearly one of Oswaldtwistle's oldest streets dating from the earliest part of the 19th century. This was housing for the operatives of the *Hippings Vale Mill* seen lower down. A poor district of Oswaldtwistle by the end of the 19th century, the area was noted for its unpleasant smells and the use of pawnbroker, *'Johnny Isherwoods'*, an Oswaldtwistle town councillor. So much trade was done that the council erected a gas lamp at the back door. The *Hippings Vale Cotton Spinning & Manufacturing Company* was a co-operative mill formed in 1861 by local tradesmen and textile operatives. The three-storey mule spinning mill was demolished by 1936.

Fire at Town Bent Colliery in March 1907. An early Oswaldtwistle fire engine is shown at the colliery, together with a crowd of people awaiting news of the miners who were underground when the pithead caught fire. Fortunately, the Town Bent workings connected with those at Aspen colliery and the miners escaped, uninjured, via this route. Town Bent Colliery was developed in 1889-92 by Thomas Simpson and was purchased by *Oswaldtwistle Collieries Ltd* in 1899. It was the town's last working colliery and closed in 1925.

Oswaldtwistle Fire Station in 1976. This was the second fire station on this site and was commissioned in November 1965. Based at Mill Hill, adjacent to the *Tinker & Budget*, the previous fire station was also located here, in a former part of *Hippings Vale Mill*, the main mill buildings being demolished in the 1930s. Sadly the fire station closed in 2003 and the service is now provided from the new station on traffic-locked Hyndburn Road, Accrington! Only time will tell whether today's service can match that provided in the past by the Oswaldtwistle-based part time crews.

The town's first ambulance, provided c1922 by the Urban District Council, pictured outside Rhyddings Park gates at the top of Rhyddings Street.

© Lancashire Library

Cook's Grocers, 358 Union Road, c1900. The shop is located opposite Roe Greave Road, adjacent to the dental surgery. In more recent years, the shop has been a sweet shop and a hairdressing salon. The gentleman and lady are believed to be Mr & Mrs William Cook. © *Lancashire Library*

Jim Mattison and his son, Jim outside the family shop at 321 Union Road, opposite the *Royal Oak* about 1929, when young Jim was 5 years old. The family lived above the shop which, in the 1920s, had no 'fridge. The fish, kept on ice, came from Creasey's on Hyndburn Road, Accrington and the meat and vegetables from Blackburn market each Friday. Jim had been a collier prior to becoming a grocer.

The main Blackburn–Haslingden road was damaged when the twenty-five-million gallon *Warmwithins Reservoir* spectacularly burst its banks on the morning of 24th November 1970. Heavy overnight rain had swelled the reservoir and mills in Oswaldtwistle took immediate precaution against flooding but, fortunately, no serious flooding occurred. The main road was closed for repairs.

Black Bull Hotel, Cocker Brook, seen here shortly before demolition in the 1930s. The settlement of Cocker Brook was swept away by the need to improve the town's water supply. Cocker Cobbs Reservoir and Jackhouse Reservoir were built by the Oswaldtwistle Urban District Council. Situated on the Haslingden, Blackburn & Whalley Turnpike Trust road, engineered by John Metcalfe, *'Blind Jack of Knaresborough'*, this was one of many inns serving travellers in the great coaching age of the late 18th and early 19th century. The road is the A677 and is known as *Haslingden Old Road*. © *Lancashire Library*

Duncan Square in March 1962. These late 18th century cottages, located at the rear of the *Palladium Cinema*, off Moscow Mill Street, were amongst the first to be built in the rapidly expanding town. The new trades also brought wealth. In 1824, Joseph Brotherhood, calico printer of Duncan Square, left £400 of personal estate plus houses and land in Oswaldtwistle and Accrington, even though he could not write. The Square also had an infant school, run by an *'Old Mrs Tattersall'* in the 1820s, 20 children being taught in the back kitchen. The *United Free Methodists* and *Swedenborgians* also established schools in the Square around that time. In the 1890s, there were reports of poor water quality, with pressures only capable of providing two hours of water per day when none was being used at *Foxhill Bank Printworks*.

Buildings on the site of the **Palladium Cinema** about 1905. Henry Cunliffe was a dealer in second hand goods and supplier of hair-restorer! The cinema was opened in 1923, some years after most of the property had been demolished.

The foundation stone of St Mary's Church on Catlow Hall Street was laid on 11th September 1897 by the Bishop of Salford, who changed the proposed name from St Oswald's to St Mary's on request. The church opened in 1898 and Father Brereton was the first priest. St Henry's R C School in Moscow Mill Street was built in 1872 and became St Oswald's School/Chapel in 1894 to serve the new mission in Oswaldtwistle. The school closed in 1964.

© *Lancashire Library*

Church and Presbytery
St. Mary's, Oswaldtwistle
Accrington, Lancs.

A group of nurses at **Paddock House** which opened in 1909 as a seminary for training priests. During the first World War it served for a time as a military hospital.

© *Lancashire Library*

Processions for both religious and other celebrations were an important part of the social calendar, particularly during the first half of the 20th century. Here we see an *Empire Day* procession on Union Road, passing the junction of Rhyddings Street in 1926. *Empire Day* was 24th May, Queen Victoria's birthday, and was celebrated throughout the British Empire, particularly in schools.

Mount Pleasant Wesleyan Band of Hope in procession, passing the junction of Havelock Street and Union Road, the site of the famous '*big lamp*' in 1910. The buildings on the left stood on the site of the present Co-op supermarket.

© *Lancashire Library*

Oswaldtwistle Fire Brigade c1900. Oswaldtwistle Fire Brigade at *Rhyddings Mill*. The mill was owned by Robert Watson. He rebuilt Riddings Hall and renamed it the *"Rhyddings"* in 1853, a name more suited to a Victorian mansion house than the name for the original farmstead. © *Lancashire Library*

The fire at Steiners at *Foxhill Bank Printworks,* 1905. The damage was estimated at £20,000. Although the works continued to be used until 1958 all the buildings have been demolished. The area was cleared and in the late 1970s became one of Oswaldtwistle's finest post-industrial developments and community schemes. Today the area is the Foxhill Bank Wild Life Nature Reserve. © *Lancashire Library*

FOXHALL BANK, FIRE, FEB 7TH 06 (A)

York Street Wesleyan Methodist procession on Union Road, passing the junction with Roegreave Road in about 1910. The photograph clearly shows ladies' fashions of the day. *Holy Trinity Free Church of England*, opened 1886, features prominently in the left background. In 1931, Rev. Thomas Cameron was appointed minister at Holy Trinity. He was ordained a Bishop in September 1951 and held his last service in Oswaldtwistle in December 1968. Oswaldtwistle had a Bishop for seventeen years – beat that Accrington! *© Lancashire Library*

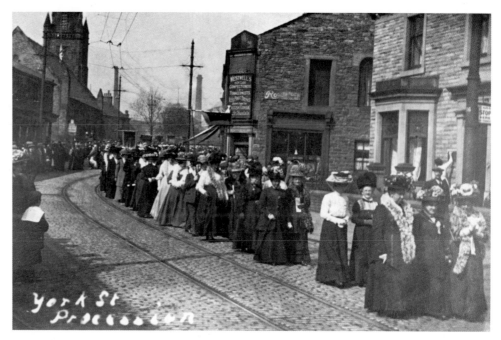

The Civic Procession to mark the death of King Edward VII passes the *Royal Oak* on Union Road. The King died on 6th May 1910.

© Lancashire Library

Cockerley Fold is one of several *'folds'* in and around Oswaldtwistle. These were early settlements dating back to the 17th century. Cockerley, along with Jackhouse, Rhoden, Town Bent, etc., became small centres for handloom weaving of wool. The Spencer family were woollen weavers at Cockerley in the 18th century.

Cocker Lumb Mill, in its moorland setting, was probably a fulling mill built in the late 18th century. Its purpose from the early 19th century until it closed in 1911 was the spinning and weaving of *'waste'*. James and John Haworth Entwistle moved from Cocker Lumb to Clifton Mill, Oswaldtwistle, in 1911. Remains can be seen in the Cocker Lumb valley, including earthworks associated with the original water wheel and the weir.

The Oswaldtwistle Co-operative Society c1900. The four-storey building on the right is the headquarters of the *Oswaldtwistle Co-operative Society*. Like most Lancashire towns the people relied on the fair and honest trading policies and practices of this organisation. The Co-ops fought to overcome the extortion of the *'truck system'*. Before Co-operatives, the textile workers were paid with tokens to purchase their groceries at the shops operated by the mills. Underweight goods, adulteration of flour with chalk and the provision of inferior quality foods often led to exploitation of the mill workers. The Co-op stopped all this and gained a place in the hearts of the poor of most northern towns. The annual share of the dividend or *'divi'* also assisted the family.

Cover of the half-yearly report and balance sheet of the Co-operative Society, 1919.

THE OSWALDTWISTLE
Co-operative Society, Limited.

Established April 25th, 1866.   Registered July 23rd, 1866.

REGISTERED OFFICE: 315, UNION ROAD, OSWALDTWISTLE.

Officers of the Society.

President: BENJ. WESTWELL.   **Manager & Secretary:** JAMES HALSTEAD, F.C.I.S.

Auditors: *EDWARD HOPE, A.C.A., Chartered Accountant & Public Auditor, and BENJAMIN WALMSLEY.

REGISTERED No. 858 R.

Half=Yearly Report & Balance Sheet

From DECEMBER 2nd, 1918, to JUNE 9th, 1919.

(212th AND 213th QUARTERS—PERIOD OF 27 WEEKS.)

Jackson, Printer, Oswaldtwistle.

St Paul's School was established in 1837 at *Busk*. The site was part of *Busk Farm*. The school continued to grow and a Sunday school began in 1882, which led to the establishment of St Paul's Church. The photograph shows a group of children at the school in about 1912, along with their teachers, Miss Mullins and Miss Fletcher. © *Lancashire Library*

A **St Paul's Church Procession** entering Union Road from Lord Street, c1910. The building on the right is the Town Hall and the cottages on the left, which continued into Union Road, were known as *Busk*. They were demolished to make way for Peel Court sheltered accommodation, which was sadly closed in 2003. Peel Court is likely to be demolished and replaced by new housing. © *Lancashire Library*

Immanuel School, New Lane, 1926. The first National School in Oswaldtwistle, New Lane was built in 1831. Until 1843 children over eight were allowed to work nine hours a day and, when not working, could attend school. In 1861, New Lane School had 125 scholars. It was not until 1876 that attendance at school was compulsory. In 1903 all children between 5 and 12 had to attend school but it was 1928 before the half-time system was abolished. When the new *Moor End Senior School* opened in 1930, the New Lane School became juniors only, but it has since closed.

© *Lancashire Library*

St Andrew's School on Kay Street at the corner of Harvey Street, 1925. The school building became a slipper manufacturing factory which is now closed. However, history repeats itself as *Hippings Vale School* was re-named *St Andrew's*.

© *Lancashire Library*

CHURCH & OSWALDTWISTLE TECHNICAL SCHOOL.   No2

The Oswaldtwistle Technical School was opened on October 7th 1911. The foundation stone was laid by Councillor Arthur Hargreaves of Moscow Mill on October 1st 1910. Arthur Hargreaves successfully ran Moscow Mills and supported and encouraged improvements in education and leisure facilities for the people of Oswaldtwistle. In 1909 he opened Rhyddings Park and on October 30th 1915 he opened the *Oswaldtwistle Carnegie Free Library*. The Technical School amalgamated with Rhyddings High School in 1961 and was the technology department of the school until 2002. The building was renovated and refurbished and is used as an assessment centre for children with behavioural difficulties.

The woodwork department of the *Church and Oswaldtwistle Technical School* c1914. The school was also known as the *Central School*. The boys shown here wear a school uniform and had been selected for this form of education by examination and school recommendation. Many would go on to engineering and higher education. Families who could not afford the uniform found themselves unable to send their child to the school even though they had *'passed'*. © *Lancashire Library*

Rhyddings Mill interior 1911, decorated for the Coronation of King George V. A weaver, dressed for the occasion, has her photograph taken amongst the bunting and decorations. The looms are silent!

Three young weavers outside *Rhyddings Mill* about 1930. Could it have been someone's birthday? The young làdy on the right was Annie Walker, the late mother of the author, Albert Wilkinson.

Paddock House in 1924 when it was a girls' convent grammar school. The house was built about 1835 by Benjamin Walmsley of Moscow Mill. The classical-style building was sadly demolished during the 1990s despite unsuccessful efforts by the Local History and Civic Societies to obtain listed building status. Some of the land was purchased as a recreation area for Rhyddings School and the rest sold and developed for housing.

Preliminary Announcement
Promoted by Peel Fold Manufacturing Co.
Proceeds for the Red Cross

A GRAND BALL

In the Town Hall, Oswaldtwistle   Friday, May 10th

J. L. Haworth's Ritz Band

Dancing 8—2 a.m.   Licensed Bar   Crystal Bowl
    Admission 2/-.   Including Refreshments

An unusual view of Frederick Street c1900, from Union Road. It shows on the right the corner of the gatehouse for Paddock House, which adjoined Moscow House, and the gates and driveway to Paddock House. This driveway was developed into the present Frederick Street in the early 20th century. The family rushing by appear to be late for something…

Union Road and Oswaldtwistle Town Hall c1915. The Town Hall was well placed in the oldest part of the town and at the heart of the community. Although many fine Victorian buildings have been lost, fine legacies of the heyday of the Lancashire textile industry remain with us as a reminder of a great age, when men and women built with opulence and strong beliefs in a great period of construction in the golden age of Queen Victoria.

R J Carter's decorator's shop opposite the Town Hall, c1910. The shop, together with that on the corner, was demolished to make way for the bank (now a gym). Mr R J Carter (left) and Moses Haworth are pictured.

© Lancashire Library

New Lane in 1900. Quieter times before it became a major route to the motorway! The wall on the left is the boundary of *New Lane Baptist Chapel*, built in 1851, since demolished and replaced by a modern building.

© *Lancashire Library*

Oswaldtwistle Co-operative Society branch No.4 was in New Lane at the junction with Clarence Street. The smartly turned-out assistants are eagerly awaiting the onslaught of customers. The premises are currently home to *Metcalfe & Tattersall*, saw specialists.

Fred Parker busy selling his ice cream outside the fire station next to the *Tinker & Budget* in the 1940s. Fred lived on Union Road, opposite St Paul's school and the sign in his window advertised that he was an auctioneer and estate agent. He also sold ice cream in the summer, and firewood and firelighters in the winter. His ice cream was made in a small building within the *Commercial Mill* yard at the end of St Paul's Street.

Yates Brothers and Whitham also had their headquarters in Commercial Mill yard and this 1940s photo shows their *Albion* lorry spick and span, ready for its nightly trunk service to London. *Spencer and Beatty*, spring manufacturers, also had premises within the yard and their products included chest expanders.

Gobbinland boundary c1910. Whilst Oswaldtwistle in general is known as *Gobbinland*, true *Gobbinland* lies above the '*big lamp*', which stood near the site of the present library. These old buildings previously occupied the site of the library in Union Road, and the '*big lamp*' probably stood to the left of this picture. The '*big lamp*' was even used as a business address by a local retailer. Their garment labels read, '*Whitton Outfitter, near big lamp, Oswaldtwistle*'.

Gobbinland boundary c1945. Accrington Corporation bus number 77, a 1931 Leyland TD1, makes its last stop before leaving *Gobbinland* for Clayton-le-Moors. The children, standing beneath the two lamps on the site of the original '*big lamp*', are about to wave the bus on its way.